Audio Access Included

CHARLIE PARKER OMNIBOOK

For E Flat Instruments • Transcribed Exactly from His Recorded Solos

To access audio visit:
www.halleonard.com/mylibrary

Enter Code
8096-9475-1336-4532

ISBN 978-1-5400-3729-9

HAL•LEONARD®

Visit Hal Leonard Online at
www.halleonard.com

Contact Us:
Hal Leonard
7777 West Bluemound Road
Milwaukee, WI 53213
Email: info@halleonard.com

In Europe contact:
Hal Leonard Europe Limited
42 Wigmore Street
Marylebone, London, W1U 2RN
Email: info@halleonardeurope.com

In Australia contact:
Hal Leonard Australia Pty. Ltd.
4 Lentara Court
Cheltenham, Victoria, 3192 Australia
Email: info@halleonard.com.au

INTRODUCTION

The solos in this book represent a cross section of the music of Charlie Parker. In presenting these solos, we hope to bring musicians closer to the true genius of "Bird"

The solos are in Eb key which means they can be read right out of the book on Alto or Baritone Saxophone. Other instruments, of course, will have to transpose. We hope to very shortly offer a condensed book of solos which will be transposed to Bb keys for Trumpet, Tenor Sax and Soprano Sax.

Most Jazz musicians have learned to play by listening to records and imitating the notes, articulations, vibrato, etc. of the masters. We encourage you to play these with the actual recording. Listen to the record first, then play through the solo slowly, gradually increasing the speed until you are at the recorded tempo Bird played it. I don't feel the idea is to try to play the solos exactly as Bird did, but rather to find phrases, articulations, scoops, turns, etc. that you feel you would like to incorporate into your own playing. By being able to see and play the actual notes, it should help speed up the learning process. Many players play like Bird but retain their own personality.

Practice with a metronome. Each day try to increase the tempo a little, all the while retaining the inflections, articulations, etc. that you would use at the slower tempo. Try practicing some of these solos with the Aebersold Play A Long records. Take a slow blues solo in F and play it with one of the records in the series that has a slow F blues, then move to a record that has a faster F blues. It is fun to work towards playing the solos with Bird along with the actual Parker recorded version.

Blues make up the largest portion of this book. Rhythm changes come next. Some compositions have the two versions recorded by Parker in separate solos. When a measure occurs without a chord symbol above it, the chord is the same as the measure preceeding it.

Most players like to analyze solos in order to find out what the musician is doing. Our ears cannot always HEAR what is happening so we slow the music down. transcribe it, analyze it, practice the licks, patterns and phrases we like best, and end up playing them in our own way on our instruments. We have put chord symbols over most all bars to enable you to analyze the notes in relation to the chord. Remember, each chord symbol represents a series of tones called a scale. Older musicians used to improvise mainly on chord tones; Charlie Parker was one of the first to broaden that to include scales **and** substitute scales. For information on scale substitution refer to the Scale Syllabus chart.* Bird loved to use the b9 over the Dom. 7th chord/scale. The Blues scale and its accompanying licks was an important part of his music, even when playing songs other than blues! When you find licks or patterns that you enjoy, practice them in several keys so the melodic phrase becomes a part of you. It should become automatic in order to really be useable in a playing situation.

Only a minimum of articulations have been put in this book. We feel that jazz, being an aural art form, is often times best imitated by listening over and over, and then playing the notes the way you hear it on the record. This might seem like the long way to do it, but experience has proven reliable. After all, who would object to listening anyway? Listening is what music is all about.

The records from which these solos are taken are listed at the top of each solo page. They are contained in approximately eight records (some are two record sets) and most all are still available. The two record sets are a bargain!

We hope you have as much enjoyment with this book as we have had putting it together.

Jamey Aebersold

* For SCALE SYLLABUS see page 143

Confirmation
VERVE 8005
By Charlie Parker

TURN PAGE

Moose the Mooche

C. PARKER 407
By Charlie Parker

Ornithology

'BIRD SYMBOLS' C. PARKER 407
By Charlie Parker and Bennie Harris

Yardbird Suite

'BIRD SYMBOLS' C. PARKER 407
By Charlie Parker

Anthropology

COLUMBIA 34831
By Charlie Parker and Dizzy Gillespie

TURN PAGE

Dewey Square

JAZZ GREATS JG-617/BLUE RIBBON 8011
By Charlie Parker

Scrapple from the Apple

BLUE RIBBON 8011/UP FRONT 171/CHARLIE PARKER RECORDS 407/SAVOY 1108
By Charlie Parker

Blues for Alice

VERVE 8010/VERVE 2515
By Charlie Parker

CHARLIE PARKER OMNIBOOK

For C Instruments (Treble Clef) • Transcribed From His Recorded Solos • Transposed To Concert Key

CHARLIE PARKER OMNIBOOK

Transposed for B Flat Instruments • Transcribed Exactly From His Recorded Solos
(Tenor and Soprano Sax, Trumpet and Clarinet)

K.C. Blues

VERVE 8840/VERVE 8010/MGM 4949/VERVE 2515
By Charlie Parker

THE PROFESSIONAL ARRANGER COMPOSER

(BOOK ONE)

By Russell Garcia

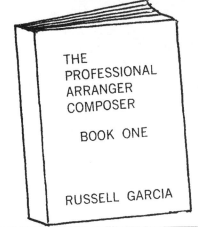

- Best selling text book used by leading universities.

- Basis for course in Practical Arranging and Composing in the professional field. For the advanced arranger.

- Endorsed by leading music educators and composers and arrangers.

AND NOW!

THE PROFESSIONAL ARRANGER COMPOSER

(BOOK TWO)

By Russell Garcia

- Discusses contemporary trends in Jazz, Pop and "Modern Classical" Techniques. New scales, chords, progressions, free improvisation, vocal effects, using tone rows in practical music, etc.

- Contains a record of many of the 169 examples and the recording of a complete score of an exciting contemporary composition by Garcia. (Musicians used are the top instrumentalists on the West Coast).

The both books complement each other!

You need both books for a complete course!

CRITERION MUSIC CORPORATION

6124 Selma Avenue, Hollywood, 90028 Calif.

Celerity

VERVE 8002/VERVE 2512
By Charlie Parker

Au Privave
(No. 1)

VERVE 8010/MGM 4949/VERVE 2515

By Charlie Parker

Au Privave
(No. 2)
VERVE 8010/VERVE 8840/VERVE 8002
By Charlie Parker

An Important Elementary
Arranging Book For Schools

Contains two records of charts in the book:

and
"Moonlight In Vermont" for full orch. and 4 examples of contemporary styles by a leading university orch.

BARNEY KESSEL says: *"This book opens the door to an arranging career for musicians. Van's first book did this for me."*

Chi Chi

VERVE 8005/MGM 4949/VERVE 8409
By Charlie Parker

TURN PAGE

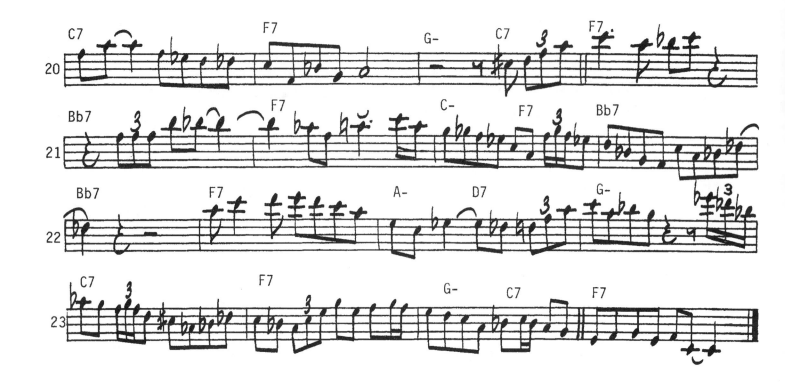

Cosmic Rays
VERVE 8840/VERVE 8005
By Charlie Parker

Cosmic Rays - cont.

Laird Baird

VERVE 8005
By Charlie Parker

She Rote
(No. 1)
VERVE 8010/VERVE 8840/VERVE 8002/VERVE 2515
By Charlie Parker

She Rote
(No. 2)
VERVE 8010/MGM 4949
By Charlie Parker

Mohawk
(No. 1)
VERVE 8006/VERVE 8840/VERVE 2501
By Charlie Parker

Mohawk
(No. 2)
VERVE 8006/VERVE 8002
By Charlie Parker

An Oscar for Treadwell

VERVE 8002/VERVE 8006/VERVE 2501
By Charlie Parker

TURN PAGE

43

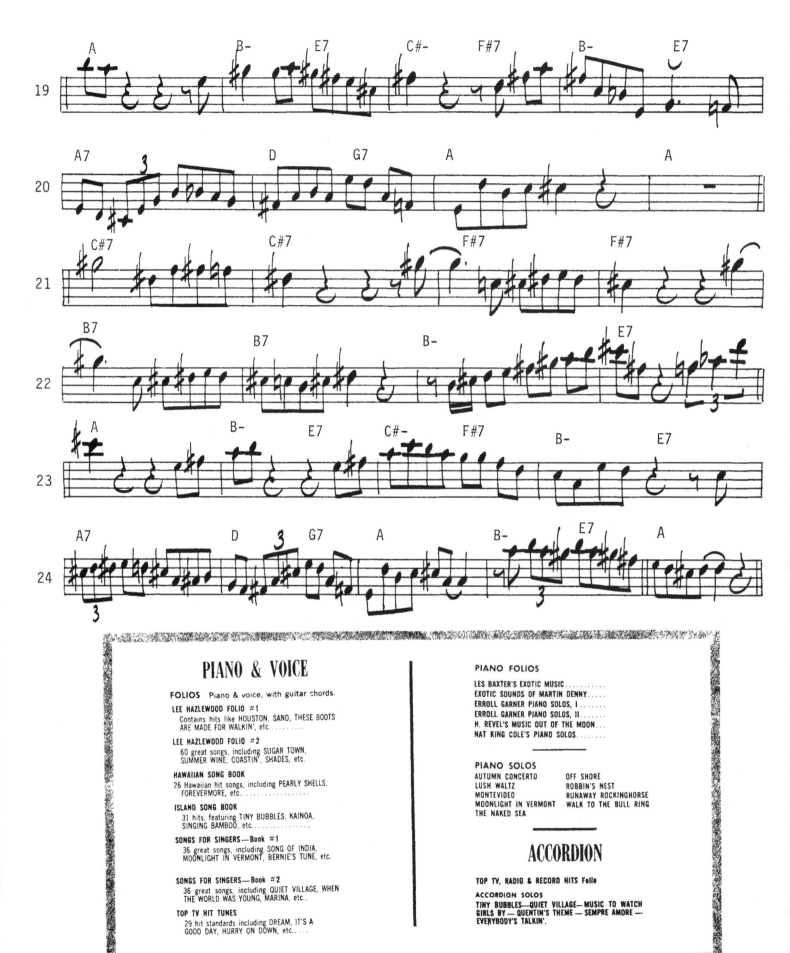

Constellation

SAVOY 2201
By Charlie Parker

TURN PAGE

Constellation - cont.

Donna Lee

SAVOY 2201
By Charlie Parker

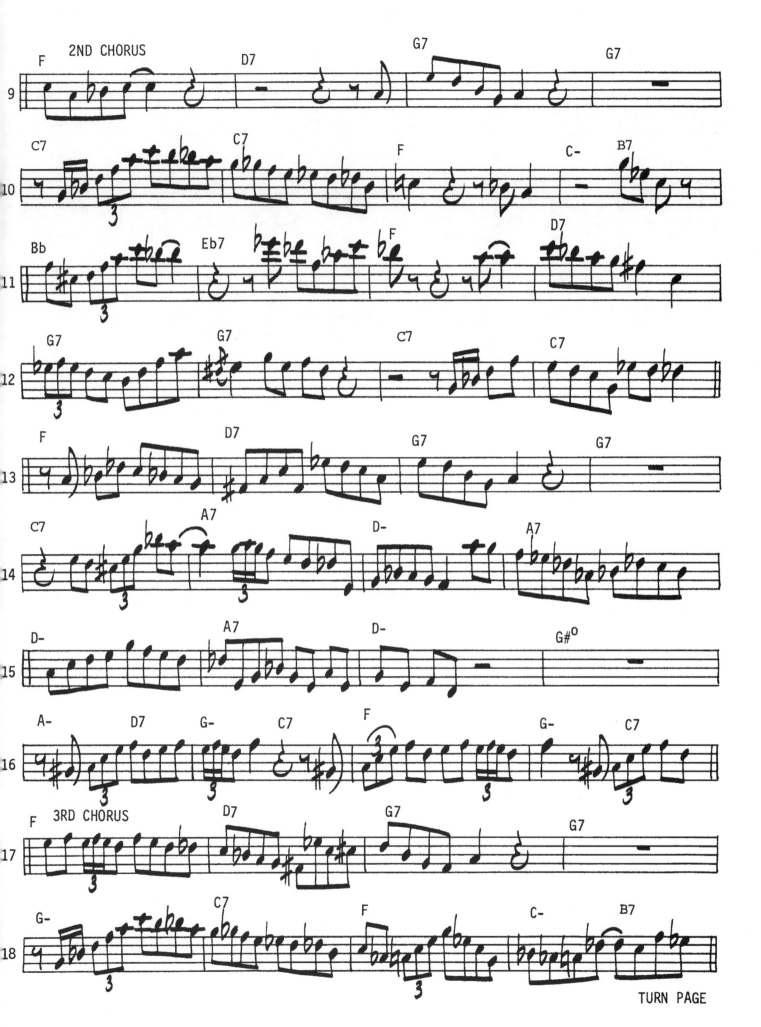

TURN PAGE

Donna Lee - cont.

Kim
(No. 1)
VERVE 8005/VERVE 8840
By Charlie Parker

TURN PAGE

ORCHESTRATIONS

SMALL ORCHESTRATIONS

MODERN SOUND SERIES

Charlie Parker's
CONFIRMATION — YARDBIRD SUITE
MOOSE THE MOOCHE — ORNITHOLOGY
SCRAPPLE FROM THE APPLE
DEWEY SQUARE

Gerry Mulligan's MULLIGANETTES
BERNIE'S TUNE — WALKIN' SHOES
NIGHTS AT THE TURNTABLE —
SOFT SHOE — FREEWAY

Illinois Jacquet's
ROBBINS' NEST
Coleman Hawkin's
STUFFY
Lester Young's
JUMPIN' WITH SYMPHONY SID

Dizzy Gillespie's
THE CHAMP

STANDARD DANCE ORCHESTRATIONS

AUTUMN CONCERTO
    (My Heart Reminds Me)
BERNIE'S TUNE
DREAM
INTERMISSION RIFF
IT'S A GOOD DAY

MARINA
MOONLIGHT IN VERMONT
OFF SHORE
QUIET VILLAGE
(AT) THE END (OF A
RAINBOW)

QUANDO LA LUNA (Small orch.)

Kim
(No. 2)

VERVE 8005/MGM 4949
By Charlie Parker

TURN PAGE

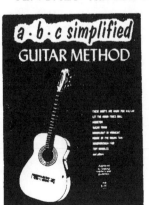

Cheryl

SAVOY 1108
By Charlie Parker

GUITAR FOLIOS

"BOOTS" FOR GUITAR
Guitar arrangements with complete parts for
Solo and Rhythm Guitar......   ....

FROM THE ROMANTIC ERA
Concert guitar solos transcribed from
Laurindo Almeida's Capitol album. music of
Beethoven, Greig, etc.. . . . .

BOSSA GUITARRA
Six solos by Laurindo Almeida with lead line
and chord symbols. . . . .

SURFIN' GUITAR
Surfing songs arranged by Jimmie Haskell
for piano solo and guitar solo. . . . . .

COUNTRY GUITAR
Hits from the Country Field. . . . .

FOLKSY SONGS FOR GUITAR (Simple to Advanced)
"MTA", "Philadelphia Lawyer", etc. . . . . .

20 GREAT TUNES FOR GUITAR (Pick Style)
39 Great Arrangements by Dan Fox, featuring
"Moonlight In Vermont". . . . .

OSCAR MOORE GUITAR SOLOS
. . . .

VENTURE FOLIOS

Book #1 — Hits like WALK DON'T RUN
Book #2 — Hits like JOURNEY TO THE STARS
Book #3 — Hits like JOSE, INSTANT GUITARS
Book #4 — Hits like DIAMOND HEAD, GRINGO

GUITAR SOLOS

AMOR FLAMENCO
BAJA
BODACIOUS & ANGRY GENERATION
BULLERIAS Y CANCION
TEHUACAN

. . . .

GUITAR BOOKS

GUITAR TUTOR by Laurindo Almeida
A complete Concert Guitar Method. . . .

THE GUITAR by Barney Kessell
A unique guide for guitarists. . . . .

Thriving from a Riff

SAVOY 2201
By Charlie Parker

60

Ko Ko

SAVOY 2201
By Charlie Parker

TURN PAGE

Red Cross

SAVOY 2201
By Charlie Parker

Marmaduke

SAVOY 2201
By Charlie Parker

Barbados
SAVOY 1108
By Charlie Parker

SHAPING FORCES IN MUSIC

By Ernst Toch

An inquiry into harmony, melody, counterpoint and form. A complete advanced music course now being used by many leading colleges as their text book.

Perhaps

SAVOY 2201
By Charlie Parker

Now's the Time
(No. 1)
VERVE 8840
By Charlie Parker

UNDERSCORE
By Frank Skinner

A complete course in scoring for motion pictures and television, featuring an
actual score that was writtern, arranged and recorded for a motion picture, with
timing sheets, orchestra sketches and orchestrations.

Now's the Time

(No. 2)

VERVE 2201

By Charlie Parker

Buzzy

SAVOY 2201
By Charlie Parker

Billie's Bounce

(Bill's Bounce)
SAVOY 2201
By Charlie Parker

Chasing the Bird

SAVOY 1108
By Charlie Parker

Blue Bird

SAVOY 2201
By Charlie Parker

Ah-Leu-Cha

SAVOY 2201
By Charlie Parker

TURN PAGE

Marmaduke - cont.

Klaunstance

SAVOY 2201
By Charlie Parker

TURN PAGE

Card Board

VERVE 2501
By Charlie Parker

Bird Gets the Worm

SAVOY 2201
By Charlie Parker

TURN PAGE

Segment

VERVE 8009
By Charlie Parker

TURN PAGE

Visa

VERVE 8000/VERVE 8009
By Charlie Parker

Passport

VERVE 8000/VERVE 8009
By Charlie Parker

Another Hairdo

SAVOY 2201
By Charlie Parker

Back Home Blues

VERVE 8840/VERVE 8000/VERVE 8010/VERVE 2515
By Charlie Parker

Bloomdido

VERVE 8840/MGM 4949/VERVE 8006/VERVE 2501
By Charlie Parker

The Bird

VERVE 2501
By Charlie Parker

Steeplechase

SAVOY 2201
By Charlie Parker

Diverse

VERVE 8009
By Charlie Parker

TURN PAGE

Diverse - cont.

Merry Go Round

SAVOY 2201
By Charlie Parker

TURN PAGE

My Little Suede Shoes

VERVE 8000/VERVE 2515
By Charlie Parker

Relaxin' with Lee

VERVE 8840/VERVE 8009/VERVE 2501
By Charlie Parker

Blues (Fast)

VERVE 8840/VERVE 8009/VERVE 2501
By Charlie Parker

TURN PAGE

Shawnuff

PHOENIX 17 JAZZ
By Charlie Parker and John "Dizzy" Gillespie

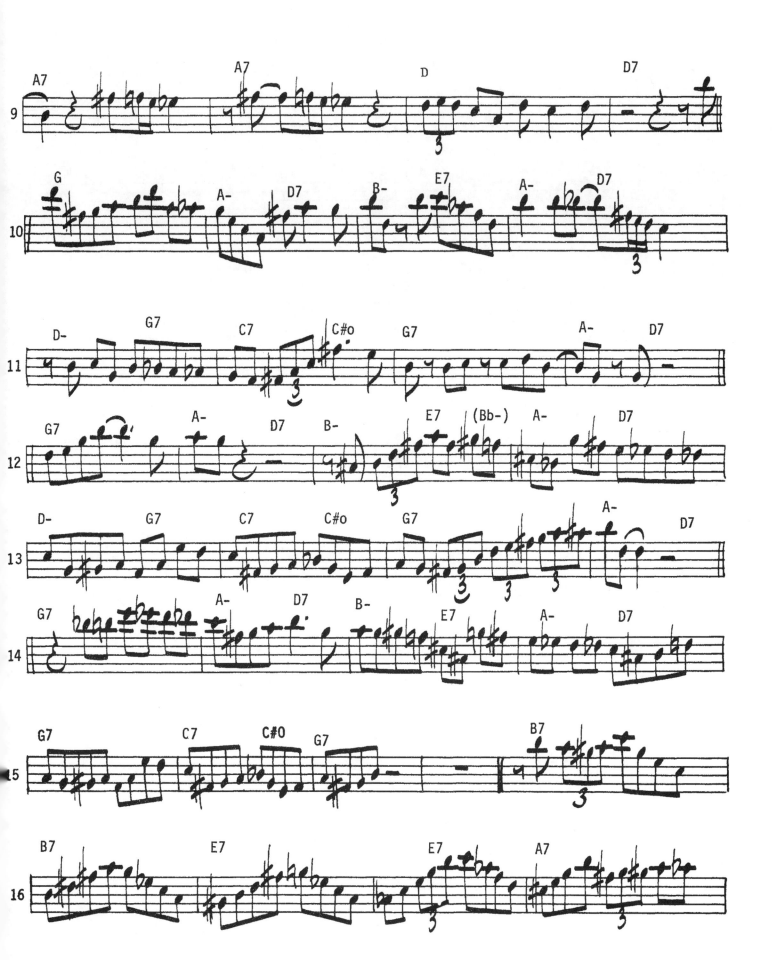

Leap Frog

VERVE 8840/VERVE 8002/VERVE 8006/VERVE 2501
By Charlie Parker

TURN PAGE

Parker's Mood

SAVOY SJL2201
By Charlie Parker

CHARLIE PARKER FOR PIANO
Recorded by The Paul Smith Trio
Cassettes available $8.98 by mail

CRITERION MUSIC CORPORATION
6124 Selma Avenue, Hollywood, CA 90028

Warming Up a Riff

SAVOY SJL2201
By Charlie Parker

TURN PAGE

Si Si

VERVE VE2-2512
By Charlie Parker

CHARLIE PARKER FOR PIANO
Recorded by The Paul Smith Trio
Cassettes available $8.98 by mail

CRITERION MUSIC CORPORATION
6124 Selma Avenue, Hollywood, CA 90028

Ballade

VERVE MGV8002
By Charlie Parker and Coleman Hawkins